POEMS
AND
WRITINGS
from a **Broken Heart**
and a **Romantic Mind**

Death is a separation that cannot be returned from; Love is not.

JACK LAMBERT

authorHOUSE

AuthorHouse™
1663 Liberty Drive
Bloomington, IN 47403
www.authorhouse.com
Phone: 833-262-8899

Published by AuthorHouse 03/29/2021

ISBN: 978-1-6655-1962-5 (sc)
ISBN: 978-1-6655-1963-2 (e)

Library of Congress Control Number: 2021905004

For Patti, still my girl
September 14, 1948–February 18, 2018

Contents

PART 3: THE DARKNESS OF LIFE

PART 4: REFLECTIONS

Preface

This is a book about what love has meant to me, both the joys and disappointments. The biggest joy came when my wife said *I do*. The biggest disappointment was the night she passed from this earth.

To try and find love again has been impossible. I thought I had found it again, only to be disappointed. The biggest thing that I have learned my entire life is that love is a gift to give and a gift to receive. If we can master this thought, we can truly do anything.

There is only one person I could dedicate this book to: my friend, my lover, my wife, Patricia Jo Shelor Lambert. She will forever be missed and can never be replaced. She stood by me through thick and thin, never complaining, never wavering.

You will be forever on my mind, for we were in love.

You were my home for me to come to.
You made me smile when I was sad.
You were my strength when I was weak.
You were my warmth in the cold night.
You were my stars in the dark sky that surrounded the moon.
You have left me now, your joy surely missed,
But your love is still here, urging me on, not letting me forget:
You will be forever on my mind, for we were in love.

There is another person I must thank, and that is Jen Adamsons. She was my editor and my guide and helped write some of what you will read. Without her long efforts, this labor of love could not have been finished. Jen, I can never thank you enough.

PART 1

Poems for Patti

A Gift

Love is a gift that, when you give it to someone, you give to yourself.
When you give love, hold that person you give it to tight.
When you give love, that kiss or embrace can express what words cannot.
When you give love, feel their heartbeat next to your body, saying you are
    mine and I am yours.
When you give love, don't be afraid, for it may come only once in your life.
When you give love, reach out to them, whisper in their ear, look into
    their eyes as you tell them that the world revolves around them and
    that you will never let them go.
Love can be cruel, love can be gentle, but above all love is a gift.

Into Each Life

Into each life there comes only one true love.
I have had mine; I miss you like crazy.
You came into my life quietly and left the same way:
Without great fanfare, without wanting anything,
But offering all that you had; always giving, never taking.
You showed me what love was really about—
Not puppy love or lust, but *love*.
That first night we dated was good beyond compare,
Quietly getting to know each other, neither demanding.
Did we both know then what the future held? I think so.
You left the same way, quietly, not demanding, without a whimper.
It was too late for goodbyes when I saw you were gone.
Lying quietly in our bed that we shared,
Did I know what the future held? I think not.
Where are you? Where have you gone?
I cannot hear your voice but in my mind. Why?
I cannot see you but in my mind. Why?
I cannot dream of you in sleep. Why?
I need the voice, I need the vison, I need the dream.
I need you.

You Loved Me

In this life, I know not for certain many things,
But I do know that you were the one who loved me.
I did not need to ask for it: you gave it freely, as I did accept it.
It was the gift most precious given, though I knew it not at the time.
Years went by, and I learned of your love and how important it was to me.
Now that you are gone, no one needs to remind me of its value,
For I now know it could not be bought, only freely given.

Strong Enough

"Are you strong enough?" she asked.
"For what?"
"To fall in love again," she said.
"Yes; I am already in love with you.
You have made my life complete, filled with joy,
With a happiness I thought was lost forever.
Are you strong enough?" I asked.
"For what?"
"To accept my love," I said. "Yes, oh yes," she whispered.

The Nights Are Cold

The nights are cold since you have left me, and I miss you.
You would keep me warm: your body close to mine,
A soft touch, a whisper in my ear, a warm embrace.
We promised that we would grow old together.
Death took you away before we could keep that promise.
You were there one second, the next you were gone.
Why, why did you have to go? Why could you not stay?
The nights are cold since you have left me, and I miss you.

Second Planet from the Left

If only I could call you to say hello, to hear your voice.
I know that I cannot: you are gone from this planet we call Earth.
Sleep comes slowly for me now: I have no one next to me;
I do not hear you whisper good night now;
I await the time that we can be rejoined in the heavens.
Let's meet at the second planet from the left. Will you be waiting?
I love you.

One More Time

One more time is all I ask for, one more night to be with you.
I still look for your face even though I know it's not there,
To watch your eyes sparkle again—I cannot, except in my mind.
To hear your voice again—I cannot, except in my mind.
To embrace you, to hold your hand—I cannot, except in my mind.
If only I could have that one more night.

Hello

To just hear you say hello is all I need to make my day.
I miss your voice; it's starting to get hard to remember it.
I ask you to come in my dreams, but you don't. Why?
Why do you stay away? I need to know that you are with me still.
I think about you every night when I am alone, remembering—
Remembering that you stayed through the bad times as well as the good,
Always supporting, never complaining, always by my side.
The light of your flame burns brightly, showing me the way.
You are never far from me, saying, "Move on; don't look back."
To just hear you say hello is all I need to make my day.

Through Your Love

You made me what I am today through your love.
When I fell, you picked me up, kissed the bruises.
When I took a wrong turn, you set me on the right path.
When I was cold at night, your embrace warmed me.
When I cried, you dried my tears.
I can say thank you no more: you have passed through the veil of death.
Yet I know you made me what I am today through your love.

I Don't Want to Live Forever

I don't want to live forever, for I would have to live without you.
You are forever by my side and in my heart and soul.
When I pray at night, you are there.
When I awake in the morning, you are there.
When I travel, I feel you in the seat beside me.
Life, I know, goes on; it will always go on with you beside me.

Goodbye

I have not said goodbye to you since you left me.

You left so quietly, so quickly, so unexpectedly.

You have moved on to our Heavenly Father; I have stayed here.

Since then, I have lived with you in my mind and heart.

You will always be in my heart, but I must let my mind rest.

I must let my mind be at peace with itself.

Until I can do this, I cannot be at peace with myself or with anyone else.

I want to move forward with life but have not.

Release my mind but not my memory; stay in my heart forever.

Help me to have peace so that I can move on in life.

Always know that you are in my heart and loved.

PART 2

Reflections of Love

The Night

The night comes again with the noise of cannons and bright lights
    flashing across the darkened sky.
Boom, boom … the sound comes ever closer, crashing down to earth
As the sky goes from dark to bright white to dark again.
The wind begins to raise its voice, ever so softly at first,
Waiting impatiently to join in the orchestra of sound that is beginning
To overcome the quiet that is supposed to be the night.
Now the wind's voice increases, no more the gentle soul that joined in
    so quietly,
But louder and louder it sings, joining the orchestra of the night.
Yet not complete is this orchestra:
One sound is missing; it can start only after the wind sings loudly.
It is not as gentle as the wind nor as loud as the sound that started the
    night's musical movement: it is the sand,
The sand that the wind lifts up from its resting place,
Throwing it in an ever-increasing crescendo of force against any object
    that seeks to stand in its way.
Now be it in minutes or hours, a note of discord sounds,

For it is the rain that starts slowly at first, sounds as though it is trying to find the right key.

So louder and louder, harder and harder the rain becomes,

Trying to outplay the other pieces of the night sky's orchestra until the disharmony, almost as it began, starts to quiet.

First the rain begins to mellow; the howl of the wind starts to lessen.

Now the sound of the beating sand begins to die.

It is in the distance now, the bright flashes of light in the sky,

Accompanied by the bass noise that sounds like cannons and finally, finally, all is at peace in God's world.

New Hope

The dawning of the day brought with it new hope.

The hope brought the beginning of a new friendship.

The friendship brought with it the closeness that comes from being with each other deep into the night.

The closeness brought with it the sincere words and joyful smiles that have not been known for longer than one cares to remember.

The words and smiles brought with them the warmth of that new dawning day.

Dare we try to repeat this process again and again, till the warmth blossoms from a bud to a flower of beauty and strength?

The Feeling, the Need, the Blessing

What is love if we don't feel it in our very being but only our heart?

Is love possible at first sight? Is love possible after one's love has passed?

What will a new love be like? Do we slip back to the old one, trying not
to let go, or jump with both feet into a new one while not forgetting?

Can we understand the difference between the two, or are we locked in
confusion between them?

Will the feelings be the same? Will the disappointments be the same and
hurt as much?

To hold another person tight is a feeling like no other. To not want to let
go is a need; to not let go is a blessing.

The journey forward is how we get from the feeling through the need
to the blessing.

Fresh Air

It is a breath of fresh air, a feeling of joy when you come into the room.

It is as though the world stops its rotation and I begin to float off to a place unknown for years.

Renewed passion takes hold as the night moon begins its trip westward.

Why does the sun chase it away so quickly? Can't it wait just one more hour before it begins that cruel trip?

From nowhere you appeared, and my greatest fear is that you will disappear back

Into the void and vanish, never to return again.

My plea is for you to stay, never leave me in the cold night alone again.

Don't let the sun chase you from this place of happiness ever.

Show Me the Way

To be close to you is both dream and reality;
To be with you is comfort, my very life.
Waiting for you to say "Come to me" is a slow, sharp pain.
The absence of your voice is a silence that is louder than an explosion.
Your reaching out for me is never quick enough—it leaves me to struggle
Between heaven and hell, not knowing for which I am bound.
I am waiting for you to show me the way.

True Beauty

What is beauty if only skin deep? Must we see only that far, or can we look
into another's soul to really see them?

What is passion if only on the outside? Must we see only that far, or can
we look into another's soul to really see them?

What is compassion if only on the outside? Must we see only that far, or
can we look into another's soul to really see them?

What is ugly if only on the outside? Must we see only that far, or can we
look into another's soul to really see them?

True beauty is deeper than skin that houses bones; it requires looking
into the soul of a person, finding what they are passionate about,
striving to see what they are compassionate about.

If you cannot do this, then all that is left is the skin that contains the
bones and too often no real beauty at all, for without passion and
compassion, there is only the ugliness.

You Make It So

The night is young, and the evening just right for you to come to me.

The breeze blows ever so softly across our bodies, intensifying the sensations of our kiss.

Passion is erupting from our embrace like lava from the lips of a volcano.

As emotions grow more intense, how can we say no, yet how can we say yes?

So much stands in the way of the many things that I want to say; new feelings want to break the bonds

That hold them tightly, old feelings saying *No, no, you can't.*

Why won't the voices in my head stop yelling, all at the same time?

Why won't they give me the peace that I so desperately need?

Then I remember that I am here with you, and all is well because you make it so.

Time

Time, time is such a cruel master, waiting ever more, waiting to become reality.

So slowly it moves forward; too slow for some, too fast for others, never at just the right speed,

Wanting to see a minute ahead so we can say or do that thing which is most correct,

Trying to get back that foolishly spent minute, the words or actions that should not have been—

While both are wanted, neither can be had.

When you are near, holding my hand, looking into my eyes, it's as though time stands still.

I am blind to future moments, and I've forgotten the one which has been.

In our embrace, I simply want time to stand still, never to move in either direction.

Moonlight

In the moonlit evening, field grass softly dances.

In the moonlit evening, leaves gently sway in the breeze.

In the moonlit evening, I see your silhouette slowly moving toward me, swaying as your body keeps time with the wind.

In the moonlit evening, I feel the wind moving me toward you, urging me to go ever faster to meet your warm embrace.

In the moonlit evening, the sweetness of your kiss brings calmness to my soul.

In the moonlit evening, the warmth of your embrace brings strength to my life.

In the moonlit evening, our love causes the heavens to explode with radiant joy.

In the moonlit evening, because you are with me, all is at peace in God's world.

Don't Curse Them

The rain storms down in torrents against whatever stands in its way,
Knowing that it's the rain's job to refresh the earth from soil to air.
Isn't that the way life is? We explode from the womb, bringing new life
    to this earth.
We grow and learn that life is more complicated than we imagined as
    children.
Then we have another explosion—with far more force, if we are lucky—
This time called love, the first to our parents and the second to lovers.
Each of these explosions, in its own way, causes our lives to be refreshed,
    as the rain does the earth.
Which is the most powerful cannot be known until we have lived our
    lives and died,
For these two earth-shattering events change us in so many ways, setting
    lifelong events in motion,
And when we pass from this earth, we will never know what we have
    touched or helped to come to pass.
Stand and rail against the wind and rain, but not against life, not against
    love:
Embrace them, live them, enjoy them, but don't curse them.

Remarkable

Oh, those remarkable eyes I briefly could see! What warmth, what sparkle
   they had.
Oh, those remarkable lips I tasted! What passion they kissed me with.
Oh, those remarkable arms that briefly held me for but a moment!
Why did you suddenly leave me alone to find my way?
Why did you suddenly say no more with so definite a word?
Knowing that there is no chance to see those eyes, taste those lips,
And feel the passion those arms hold is almost more than I can bear.
Remarkable will be the memories that I hold;
Remarkable will be the loss that has come to be,
For you are remarkable and unforgettable.

Second Greatest Gift

Love is the second-greatest gift that God has given to man,
But when that gift is lost, what do we do?
Do we search for a new meaning to life, or do we go into a shell?
When we are able to find a new love, it is a great blessing.
What do we do when that one is also lost?
Is the devastation as great as the first loss?
Is retreat from the world more likely?
I stumble to answer these questions. I know it makes it harder to trust,
    to love again,
But I do know to live a life without love is a terrible life, a hollow life.

Soaring

I could fly when you were with me, fly high as I wanted to.
To soar in the sky beside you was all that I needed, all I asked for.
But now you are gone, soaring far above, where I can never go—
Soaring not by yourself, but with the angels in God's heaven.

The Night Is Quiet

The night is quiet because you are gone.
The night is quiet without your voice.
The night is quiet without your laughter.
The night is quiet and cold without your warm embrace.
The night is quiet, and my bed is empty without you there.
The night is quiet; do not let it be long before we are together again.
The night is quiet because I miss you.

Your Life

I want to be there for your life, good or bad.
I want to be there for your life for every moment.
I want to be there for your life, for every joy, for every tear.
I want to be there for your life, for every passion, every hate you might
     have.
I want to be there for your life, to see what you see, to hear what you hear.
I want to be there for your life, to warm you when it's cold, to bring you
     a breeze when it's hot.
I want to be there for your life because you are my life.

Wanting and Waiting

Why does the rain pour and sound loud on the roof?
Why does it sound as though the tears come from heaven?
The thunder sounds as though the heavens are mourning.
The winds rustle the tree leaves in unison. Is it possible the angels are
     crying?
Why this sound of despair, what is the cause? Could it be because you
     are not here?
Could the heavenly bodies know of my wanting, waiting for you to come?
I know only that you are not near, and the heavens will not be still till
     you are.

You Are My Now

You are my now; I do not care for tomorrow or what was yesterday.

Your tears are mine to share, your joys mine to celebrate.

Not to be with you leaves sorrow in my very being.

You need not try to seduce me—you have me already.

When God thought to bring you into my life, I did not know

The happiness you would bring when you were with me nor the sadness
  when you were not.

My happiness is nothing without you to share it, my sorrows too much
  to bear

Without your shoulder for my weeping head to rest on.

Never, never go away: the sadness that would bring would be unbearable.

You Are My Heroine

You are my heroine in life, full of a spirit that nothing can stop.

You are my heroine in life, with a smile and kind word for all you encounter.

You are my heroine in life, overcoming setbacks that cause the rest of us to quit.

You are my heroine in life, because you see the good in people and not the bad.

You are my heroine in life; to be with you is a privilege that I don't want to lose.

You are my heroine in life, full of a spirit that nothing can stop.

Never Stop Bringing Your Sweetheart Flowers

Never stop bringing your sweetheart flowers; it is a visual show of love.
Never stop that whisper of love in the night; they need to hear it.
Never turn away from your lover at night in bed; they need to see you,
For it says "Come to me, for I am yours alone."
Always let your hearts beat together as one—so often we forget.
Be your lover's beginning and ending each morning and night.
To travel the road alone brings much sorrow; to travel it together, as one,
    brings great joy and happiness

This Season

I needed you not in the spring and summer of my life, but I need you now.
This is the winter of my years, and you have come into it.
Why it is for such a short time, I do not know.
What can I provide for you that you have not already gained?
Yet you freely give to me from your love and ask for nothing.
I can only hope that this season of my life will last a long time.

Will You Forget Me

Will you forget me when I am gone, when you no longer can feel my kiss, my passion?

Will you forget me when I am gone, when you no longer hear my heart beat with yours at night?

Will you forget me when I am gone, when you can no longer laugh at my silly jokes?

Will you forget me when I am gone, when I no longer hold your hand tightly on long walks?

I will miss you, because you have been my life, the one love that I cherished above all others.

Dream

Everyone needs a friend; everyone needs someone to love.
You were to be mine, and I yours.
But someone woke me up from my dream too soon.
Come back and stay with me; let me dream again.
If that is the only way I can be with you, I will see you there.

Alone in My Thoughts

I am alone in my thoughts because you are not with me.

You have said goodbye, and I know not why.

My thoughts betray my emotions like a coming storm:

I can hear the thunder in my mind and am waiting for the lightning to
appear.

You came into my life with a whirlwind of excitement in your kiss,

Your embrace carrying me to a place I had never been.

Now your leaving has taken me to a loneliness unknown before.

Leave me, this flood of emotion, for I need to live my life in peace.

I Was Not the First

Was I the first to have kissed your lips? I was not.

Was I the one who held your hand on that first walk? I was not.

Was I your first embrace? I was not.

Was I the one who watched the stars or the sunrise with you that first
time? I was not.

Was I your first love or the one who shared your love first? I was not.

All these firsts I missed, but I am here now, wanting to share your love
and your life for the rest of your life.

I will not miss any more.

True Love

I was lucky to have known the meaning of true love, for I have had my
  great love in life and lost her.
She was my friend, my lover, my partner, my wife.
How do you find that second love? Where do you look, and how do you
  know if or when it happens?
You haven't the time left nor the same enthusiasm in life to look.
We become set in our ways through the years, sometimes to the point of
  being unwilling to change.
Those who have lost understand; those who have not may say they do but
  cannot truly understand.
We go on, some satisfied with their life, others searching for a second
  chance at love but never finding it.
Is it because of shadows from the past? Not that you want to replace a
  memory, but they can haunt your very being.
Perhaps we push too hard, fearing that time will run out before we find it.
Society has changed from moving slowly into a relationship to instant
  gratification—"I like you, let's live together."
That is not how relationships are made nor how they stay together.
But the question remains. Do you have the answer? I do not.

Life Complete

To just be in your presence should be enough, but it's not.
To only see your smile should be enough, but it's not.
To only hear your voice should be enough, but it's not.
For you are all things to me, and I need all of these things from you
To make my life complete.

Mystery

You are like the mystery of life to me, waiting to be understood,

Not backing away, but ever moving forward, with a desire to see over the next horizon, never back to the hill behind.

The lust for life that fills your spirit is a joy to watch; it springs out of your soul.

The world is so far behind that it can no longer see you ahead but simply follows your trail.

Why did it take so long for me to find you? Couldn't I see past the shadows to the flowers?

If you ever leave, the shadows will block the sunlight from the flowers, and they will wilt before my eyes, never to be seen again.

Stay with me, for the sun has brought the flowers, and the flowers have brought beauty into my life.

I want to stay in its warmth till I leave this world. Will you stay alongside me?

Don't Close Your Heart

When you see me, don't close you heart to me.
See me for who I am, not for what you want me to be.
If I could, I would be all the things that you desire, but I cannot.
I can be only what I am and bring to you what I have.
Going forth, you will be my reality, my life.
Your dreams will be mine to try to fulfill and make come true.
When I fall short, forgive me; I will try again, not because I must, but
    because I want to.
When you see me, don't close you heart to me.

Side by Side

You have let me become part of your life, on a journey to a place I have
    not been to before.
Side by side, holding hands, we will make this journey to places we do
    not know.
It can be frightening, this journey in life, but I have you to be by my side.
I offer myself as a guide and shelter from the storms that life can bring.
After the storm, I will rest in your arms, grateful for your gentle strength
    and comfort.
We will go into the winter of our lives knowing that nothing can separate
    us, only make us stronger.

Our Difference

I will never show you anything but my true face and feelings. Will you
   for me?
I will share the secrets of my life, both good and bad. Will you for me?
I will not be a stranger that only spends nights and disappears by day.
   Will you for me?
In the sadness of life, I will offer you a place of comfort. Will you for me?
In the joys of life, I will rejoice with you. Will you for me?
That is the difference that we will show the others.

My Present

As I hold you close, I feel your heartbeat and am thankful that this is my
   present from you.
May there never be a reason for you to go away. I need you near always.
You are my reason to breathe, to wake in the morning, to dream at night.
Because of you I have joy; when I walk into a room with you there,
It's as though I'm walking on air, as if I could touch the moon and the
   stars.
Never go and take that from me, for I fear the world would end if you left.

More Than He Did

Let me be the one to love you more than he did.
Let me be the one to hold you close while the storm rages all around us.
Close your eyes and hold on tight, for I will watch for danger.
Our journey will not be smooth, for one never is,
But we will survive within ourselves, each providing comfort for the
other,
Each searching for that shore that provides a respite from the storm of life.
Let me be the one to love you more than he did.

Forgiven

It is not all forgiven, for there is nothing from you to forgive:
You were perfection and flawless to my weak ineffective ways.
I was unable to fulfill your needs and expectations.
I wanted too much and provided too little.
If only I could turn back time, now that I know what a fool I was.
If only I could have seen that my boldness would lead to this downward
    path,
With my heart reaching for any hold to stop the out-of-control tumbling
    spiral.
Still, they say nothing ventured, nothing gained, but how could they be
    so cruel?
For surely they know the heartache that failure is sure to bring.

Take That Chance

As I wander among the clouds of my sleep, I wonder what your dreams are.
Are they like mine, do you see the sun peeping through with its warm
    light
Are your dreams of past loves or cold nightmares
Has anybody told you it's alright to let go and love again just for love's sake
Are the cold nightmares stopping you from taking that giant leap of faith
    just for loves sake
I want to scream it out loud, it's okay, let go, hold back nothing, let passion
    flow
As the clouds slowly yield to the blue sky, close your eyes once more and
    take that chance
Take that chance for no other reason than just love

Love Is a Strange Thing

Love is a strange thing; it can be won or lost.

Love is a strange thing; it can be given or taken away.

Love is a strange thing; it can be hidden or revealed.

Love is a strange thing; it is complicated yet simple.

Love is a strange thing; sometimes you just have to jump in with both feet and take a chance to find that mysterious, majestic, unequaled feeling.

Love is a strange thing; it is not possible to always stand back and be an observer. Search for it; take a chance, for tomorrow may never come.

Love is a strange thing, it may come only once or it may come a thousand times.

Love is a strange thing, but above all it must be found.

Push Forward or Fall Back

Push forward, or fall back.

To boldly push, risking the loss of what has been found, or to cautiously advance, knowing that this too could result in loss;

To combine the two to find a path forward, so as to avoid a loss;

Moving forward by faith, searching for what is there, without losing what is here—

Push forward; to stand still or retreat are not options.

To die in battle brings glory; the other way, shame. So I shall explore the future with laughter and joy.

One Less Soul

What is the world with one less soul to play with?
Is it a great loss to society, or simply a space that can now be taken up by
a more useful soul?
What is the world with one less soul to play with?
Who would grieve this loss? Who would say he was my friend or lover?
What is the world with one less soul to play with?
Is the world not better if this space is taken over by a new, more talented
soul?
What is the world with one less soul to play with?
I say it is a sad place; it is a loss for all human kind to mourn.
What is the world with one less soul to play with?
A sad place to live until we know why, and it's only by being that one less
soul that we truly learn the reason.

Take the Chance or Stay the Course

As the sun's fingers claw their way upward through the silent darkness
that is the night, is there but a glimpse of hope that springs forth?
As the light slowly brings forth that welcome pink that begins to chase the
darkness away, is it the hope of a new day, or just the false beginning
before a storm?
Do we as humans ever really know what the new day will bring or what
new relationships will hold?
Do we take the chance or stay the course? One leads to surprises and new
promise but also to disappointments; the other to the same as before.
Why should we take the chance? Why risk rejection and pain when we
need not?
Why be made the fool when we are already jokers enough?
It's a mystery to me that can never be unraveled, for if it was, it may be
the end for all of us.

Fear

Fear of the found, lost before its value can be realized—
Is that what we are afraid of?
Why?
Is it the unknown that we are afraid of?
Why?
Is it the fear of the unfulfilled that we are afraid of?
Why?
Is it the fear of the past that we are afraid of?
Why?
How can we lose what we do not truly possess?
How can we fully possess what we fear?
Is the fight to possess something more powerful than the fear of losing it?
Why?
How do we justify one emotion over the other?
Why?
God says to love thy neighbor as thyself, yet so often we fear to.
Why?
Are we so insecure and self-centered that we are afraid to do this?
Why?
Why can we not answer any of these questions?

Call My Name

Why didn't you call my name when we passed?
Was it the new fellow who held your hand so tight?
I wanted to say hello, but you looked away so as not to see me.
That was more painful than the words you said when you slammed the
    door.
I turned after you went by and watched you disappear into the darkness.
And I wondered, as I watched, *Why didn't you call my name when we*
    passed?

Touch the Ground

Do your feet touch the ground, or do you float above it?
The feet provide stability for the body whole.
They must touch something beneath them.
Those that float go about their lives with no real feelings.
They feel that they are above the fray, above the fight to survive.
Those that feel the solid earth know the blisters of life.
They stub their toes on the rocks that cause us to switch paths.
Those that float often stay on the same path; there is nothing that causes
    them to change paths.
May your feet always touch the ground, with that occasional stumble on
    a rock that causes you to switch paths.

Human or Alien?

If we are not human, then do we become aliens?
If we lose our humanity and cannot find our way back again, what is left
    of us?
Are we transforming into creatures that are so ugly, so grotesque, that we
    do not recognize ourselves?
Do we then become alien to those who know us, and to ourselves as well?
What is left in life at that point when there is no feeling but despair and
    coldness?
If we are not human, then do we become aliens?

Solitude

A broken heart starts a night of silence and tears.
Somewhere a girl has said no to her boyfriend,
And now he knows not what to do:
No more sweet kisses, no more embraces of passion,
No one to hold his hand on the journey of life,
Only solitude and tears tonight.

Strength and Desire

The frost will be upon the ground by morning as the cold air moves ever
so slowly down from the north,
But I cannot wish against it, for it means that you will be in my arms
tonight,
Your kiss and embrace bringing tenderness and excitement to my weary
body.
For I have waited a lifetime to be with you tonight and feel your warmth,
your fervor and comfort.
For this gives me strength to rise and fight another day, gives me the
desire to see what the new day will unfold at my feet.
When you call to me and say, "Come, I am here," I want to stay long after
you tire of me and say go,
Never wanting to leave the tender touch of your embrace, never wanting
to let go for fear of losing you.
'Tis but a dream in the air, but if it were possible, your step would be my
step, your breath would be mine, and what you feel I would feel too.
Winter's crisp breath is closing in, and I will not see you tonight except
in my dreams,
But if I could, all would be at peace in the world and in my life.

If

If I were but a young man, I would have my strength back,
Back to do things that now only are in my imagination.
To begin again is the great fantasy; if only
I would choose my same love all over again,
For she gave me a life of love that money could not buy.
She gave me sons who became strong men.
My joys were hers, my tears hers also.
Separated by death we are, still together in my heart forever.

Ceaseless Pleas

Oh God, my God, I have tried to call to you for relief from my woes.
I have tried not to forsake your teachings and commands.
I asked for your grace and forgiveness when I failed.
I have tried to come to you in my prayers; I get silence from you.
All things I know are in your time, but my time runs low.
My needs are little this late in life, for you have blessed me immensely,
But since you took my love to you, loneliness has been my companion.
Is this my curse for not always obeying you—to be alone?
I cannot go to sleep at night nor wake without this thought.
Hear my ceaseless pleas to you, I pray.

Seasons

Oh spring, my spring, where have you gone?
You were my beginning, my learning years.
My mother and father taught me as best they could.

Oh summer, my summer, where have you gone?
That was my time to grow, to explore life.
My wife loved me and gave us sons.

Oh fall, my fall, where have you gone?
This was my time to savor the gains of summer;
This was my time to prepare for the coming winter.

Oh winter, my winter, you are here now!
This is a time for family, but they are far off.
This is a time to gaze back and see all that was.
This is a time to wonder why I choose the path I took.
Change that path, I would not … perhaps a step or two.

Could, Would, Should

I could have, if I had known. I would have, if you had asked. I should have
but didn't.
Why do we let ourselves get caught in this web of denial?
I could have, if I had known—why didn't you look to see if you could help?
I would have, if you had asked—why didn't you ask, why didn't you look?
I should have but didn't, because you didn't look, you didn't ask.
Many things are left undone because of this. Make a point to look and ask.
Then you can say *I did it*, not that you should have.

The World Has Gone Crazy

The world has gone crazy and is on fire. I am insane.
Will you join me before the world destroys itself?
Or will you be the last holdout refusing to believe there is a fire,
Refusing to believe reality, only seeing the fantasy that is shown on
television?
Do you not see the hunger, the pain, the disease that has overtaken
society?
Are you content to sit by and hide from all of this?
Grab a hose and turn on the water—not to protect what is yours alone,
But to beat back the fire that is consuming all of us.

Will the Sea Miss Me

Will the sea miss me when I'm gone, never more to sail its deep blue
waters?

Will the sea miss me when I'm gone, never to pace the deck that brought
me violence in war, bounty taken, and a place to lay my head?

Will the sea miss me when I'm gone, when I can no longer sail into port
to tell of my crew's adventures?

Will the sea miss me when I'm gone, when they drink that final salute,
fire that last cannon?

Will the sea miss me when I'm gone? I think not, for that will be my
resting place,

Over the side to the deep six, to be with those that have gone before me
and rest eternal.

Midnight Comes

Midnight comes again, its fingers of darkness all enveloping.

Into each life it comes at least once, leaving you with a sense of being alone.

To some it is but a brief moment of pain; to others it lasts and lasts until we can find the strength to fight it—and it is a fight, sometimes to the death.

The strength comes from many sources: sometimes the Divine, but many times from someone unexpected, someone we haven't met yet.

It's at the moment of defeat that we often find a reason to go on, a reason to live again.

When we find that reason, it's not to make us forget what happened, but to see that there is hope, hope for a new joy, hope for a new love, hope for life.

Nighttime

As the daylight fades, overtaken by the long fingers of the coming night,

The breeze softly brings the frosty air down from the hilltops toward the ground.

The flowers fold their petals, preparing for the chilly night.

The smell of burning wood arrives from the fires that will keep us warm.

Inside, soft music plays as children don their pj's, getting ready for bed.

Now that the night is quiet, the parents settle in for time alone together.

As their warm bodies become one with desire, the night sounds are heard:

The owls and the night birds sing, and all is at peace in God's world.

Bed of Dreams

It is cold and windy in my life since you left me.
The bed has become my friend; I can be with you there, in my dreams.
It protects me from the reality of life without you.
I always thought that I would be the one to leave first, not the one still
    here.
It is not the rain that falls but tears my cheeks feel.
Let the world be left to its own sorrows.
Come, join me in my sleep once again.

Light of Day

The darkness gets deeper and darker without you here.
You were a mystery to me while you were here,
Never solved, never unraveled, always near and yet far away.
With me you will always be, in my dreams, in my prayers,
Deep in my soul, deep in my heart, always dreaming of you.
I know that the light of day got brighter when you got to heaven.

Gone from My Side

You are mine, and I am yours as I lie here tonight.
You may be gone from my side but never from my heart.
I can still feel you as I go on without you.
You are in the heavens, in the stars that I see.
You watch me from there, and if I could be with you, I would.
Wait, oh wait for me: I will join you to shine down on those we left behind.

Yesterday, Today, Tomorrow

You were not with me yesterday; you may not be here on the morrow.
But today you are with me … and yet you are not.
You are here but far away; I can touch you, but do you feel that touch?
I could stay with you till I leave this earth, but could you stay with me?
Your soul is restless beyond understanding.
Your passion seduces, your kiss warms my heart, but somehow you are
    not here.
How can I traverse the distance between us? I find no way.
I may cry tears when you are gone—I cannot say,
For yesterday has become today and will be gone when tomorrow arrives.

Dream or Fantasy

Are you a dream, a fantasy without a reality?
It frightens me to think that you are not real.
If this is a dream, let me stay asleep as long as the dream stays with me.
If I awake, you may be gone—that I could not bear.
You are that place I never dared to go before.
You have taken over my thoughts, my life, my very soul.
You are where my mind and body belong.
I have never known love this strong, and now I want to know:
Are you a dream or a fantasy?

Broken Lifeline

You have broken the lifeline that held me to you.
You said it was my insecurities; I say it's your unwillingness to accept me
    as I am.
You will not change for me; I don't want you to.
As much as I try, I cannot seem to change enough for you.
Your life is busy, mine boring, and perhaps that is the problem.
You cannot slow down, and I can't speed up enough for you.
Is there a future for us? Only time and fate will tell.

One Rose

I know that I don't have to bring you flowers, but would one rose hurt?
You say there is no need; I say there is—
Not because you need it, not because you ask for it, not because I must,
    but because I want to.
Just one rose: what can it hurt? It is because I care that I bring it to you,
Just one rose to show you I have not forgotten what you are to me,
Just one rose because I want to.

Don't Ask

Don't ask me why I need you like I do.

Don't ask me why I need you like I do—it could be the joy you bring to my life.

Don't ask me why I need you like I do—it could be your smile that I see.

Don't ask me why I need you like I do—it could be the way you hold my hand.

Don't ask me why I need you like I do—it could be the laughter that you share.

Don't ask me why I need you like I do—it could be the tenderness of your embrace.

Don't ask me why I need you like I do—it could be the way you share your world.

Don't ask me why I need you like I do, but I do.

Gently

Gently the rain falls from the sky to the ground.

Gently your voice comes to me, saying *Listen* to my every emotion.

Gently you take my hand and lead me from room to room in your mind.

Gently you hold me tight, kiss my lips, and say *Come to me*.

Am I asleep and still dreaming? Can it really be you who lies beside me and says *Awaken*?

I do not want to wake; you may be gone, and I will be alone again.

I cannot bear that nightmare; let me sleep and dream of you.

When I Leave This Earth

When I leave this earth, will you miss me as I will miss you?
When I leave this earth, I will only talk to you in dreams,
Dreams of what was in the past, not as we once dreamed, the future.
What was once held so dearly now is no more.
I will never again hold your hand, never again embrace you.
Will you miss that as I will? Will you reach out, not remembering I am
    not there?
In the good times and the bad times, we stayed together as one,
You by my side, never behind, never in front, always together,
Together no more. I bid you to live your life as I knew you would want
    me to,
For life on this earth does not end for the living, only for the dead.

Useless Dialogue

It is a quiet that you don't want to hear:
A silence with no voices, no noise, no traffic.
I cannot speak, for there is no one to listen.
You nod and smile, but where are you?
Pretend as you will, your mind is not here.
You could be a thousand miles away in your thoughts—
Those I cannot see, I cannot hear.
When did we stop our talking to each other? I know not.
Was it all of a sudden or over a period of time that
Our voices became distant to each other?
Is that what you want, to stop this useless dialogue,
This babble that you call words that neither listens to?
So be it: go back to your thoughts; I will go to mine.

Games

Gone you are, but even for a short time it is too long.
You fly away to play, and I am left waiting for your return.
Will there be a day when you don't return?
Is your wanting to play more than your wanting for me?
I can only wait and hope that day never comes
And that you're not playing a game with me.

X Factor

If you were in a math equation, you would be the X factor.
You *are* the X factor, the unknown in my life.
You are a fresh, new factor in my equation, full of energy,
Full of passion, full of the very essence of life.
When I am with you, my spirit is renewed.
When I am away from you, you are in my thoughts.
At night, you are my only dream.
You are my X factor, and I cannot figure you out.

When It Bites

How do you know when it bites, when you get that unmistakable feeling?
Where will you be when you stop to take a second look at what you
    just saw?
Will it be in the pit of your stomach? Will it be in your chest?
Will your first thought be, *Wow, this can't be happening to me*?
Will you be young, old, or somewhere in-between?
Will it happen only once? Twice? Or will it happen over and over?
Love is a perplexing thing: you don't know where it comes from or how
    often.

The Bell Tolls

You are gone from my life, and the bell tolls.
For only a short time you were with me.
What happened to you I know not.
Your love was not real, even though your passion was hot.
You cooled quickly to me, while I was still in dreamland for you.
I was not on your social level, was not on the A-list.
Family and friends I did not meet; were you ashamed?
But still I wanted to be with you, even for that brief moment of life.
Somewhere in my mind you will live, for I cannot forget you.

You Will Miss Me

You will miss me, not like I will miss you, but when a storm comes, a storm with lighting and thunder, that will be the time you will think of me.

You will miss me, but not like I will miss you, the warmth of your embrace, the passion of your kiss, your laughter, your gentleness.

You will miss me, but not like I will miss you; you are a rock upon the sand, steady, fighting against the tide, not being swept away.

You will miss me, but not like I miss you, for I am like the sand being swept away with the tide, not knowing where the tide will take me.

You will miss me—not like I will miss you, but you will.

Good for You

I would be good for you, but you would be better for me.
We can only give to the other what is most precious: love.
Can you see your way to doing this? I know I can.
I bring myself to you and offer this as my gift, unreserved.
Will you bring yourself to me and offer the same?
Do not say you can if you have doubts; I have none.
I would be good for you, but you would be better for me.
On those cold winter nights when our embrace could warm the other,
I will feel no sorrow for being there with you.
Will you also feel none for being there with me?

Where Does That Leave Us?

I said yes, you said maybe, so where does that leave us?
"I want to move on," you said. Not so fast—where does that leave us?
"I don't have much time left in life," you said. Of course you do—where
does that leave us?
I must move on, you said. Stay awhile—where does that leave us?
"In life we have to make a choice," you said. Why, and where does that
leave us?
"I need to love again," you said, but it's so quick. "I know," I said.
I closed the door and slowly walked away.

Trees and Love

Love is like a tree: at first it is small, barely making it out of the earth, and love,

Love starts the same, barely making it out of lust.

The tree starts to grow taller reaching for the sky, and love,

Love does the same; it grows taller reaching for the sky.

The tree branches then spread out in the springtime bloom, and love,

Love blossoms out, and if we are lucky, blooms into marriage.

The tree grows large and supports many branches, and love,

Love grows the same, supporting a growing family.

The tree then falls or gets cut down, but seeds from it start the cycle again, and love,

Love gets cut down with death, but if lucky, seeds from it start the cycle again.

Love does not, cannot die unless we let it.

Sweet Gift

In the middle of the night, I want to reach out and touch you,
But I dare not. I just lie there watching you, listening to you breathe,
Watching in the darkness, looking at your beauty, wondering how, why—
How I got so lucky, why you choose me from all you had to pick from.
I do not deserve this present, this love that you bestow on me,
But I am joyful in my acceptance and will try to return your sweet gift
    every waking moment.

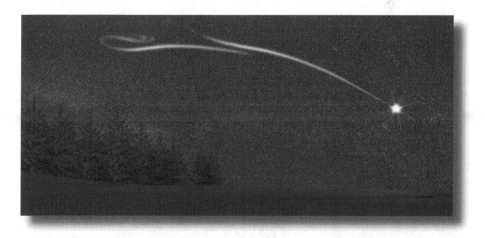

Here on Earth

The darkness comes on out of the east, slowly, methodically overtaking
    the light,
Low in the sky at first, then higher, moving ever faster as it erases the last
    of the day.
Soon after, the moon in its glory makes an appearance, with its pale light
    brightly silhouetting the horizon.
Then the first twinkling orbs of white light begin to appear.
What a wondrous sight of beauty they project overhead as the lovers
    watch!
I told her I would take her to the moon someday. I failed.
As I looked into her eyes, I realized she had no need for it.
I had no need either, for I had all I needed here on earth.

I Searched for You

Will you be the love that I have searched for? Will you be mine?
The journey will not be straight, will not be swift, but oh, how I want to
    take it.
This road that we are on is rocky; it has many curves in it.
It will take us to places that neither of us has ever been.
I have searched to find a heart that will beat with mine.
Lying next to you, I feel yours beating in chorus with mine.
I have searched for you: be my love that never goes away.

Alone Again

First time, what was it like? Was it unexpected, was it awkward?
When I saw you for the first time, I knew not the road that we would take.
That first date, I was not prepared for you as we lay together, your
    silhouette against the soft moonlight breathtakingly beautiful.
I thought, *This is what heaven must be like*, this feeling of your enchantment.
The quiet beauty of the night was not long enough; why did it have to end?
"When can we be together again?" I asked. "Never," she quietly replied as
    she silently prepared to leave.
She did not speak as she closed the door, and I'm alone again.

Again

Midnight, and you are not by my side—again.
You say it is my fault, but offer no explanation as to why.
I said that I was ready to come to you, now.
You said, "What is the hurry? We have plenty of time." But do I?
I am getting older and am looking for my last love, true.
I will wait till the new year is over to see.
Midnight, and you are not by my side—again.

I Will Know

I will know when you will be with me for my fall.

I will know when you will be there for my winter.

These are the only two seasons that remain for me to be with you.

Shadows of the past will not be unseen or forgotten, for they were my
    spring and my summer.

What surprises and joy will the fall and winter bring for us I cannot even
    begin to imagine.

Before I saw you, I was lost, stumbling along uncertain where to go, not
    knowing what to do.

You accepted me like a breath of fresh air flowing into my body.

I want to hold my breath forever, never to exhale, never to let you go.

I will know when you will be with me for my fall.

I will know when you will be with me for my winter.

I will know you will be here for life.

I Feel Fine

I feel fine when she's around me; she is like the beginning of life.

It's like beauty at the beginning of a new day:

The pink dawn light, white fluffy clouds, and soft breeze that tells me
she has come.

She brings with her the warmth of a spring day and the sparkle of the
flames in a fall night's fire.

When she says hello, it is like an orchestra playing a soft love melody.

When she says, "You're silly," I smile and silently laugh.

I eagerly wait for her to say, "Come here, you"; it is like no other phrase
I hear.

Why she goes away I cannot say, but the wait is long for her return.

Quickly return to my life, for it is a shell without you.

Ready or Not

Time, oh time, where have you gone? Have you flown away with the
cuckoo?

Time, oh time that I've wasted, why have you let me do so?

Could you not have been more of a friend and slowed it down just once?

If I could, I would mount a majestic steed and joust with you to halt your
march.

I will no longer waste what you have given to me.

I want to rejoin those that dream, I want to rejoin life.

If you will just set me free from the ropes that bind my spirit, I will soar
to the highest mountain, across the longest plain, searching for the
next chapter of life.

It is with a joyful heart that I will leave you, not knowing where this new
adventure will lead, but willing to open my life to it.

Watch out, life: ready or not, here I am with passion. Let the adventure
begin!

Move On

"Move on with life," she said. "But how?" I asked.

"Move on with life," she said. "But why?" I asked.

"Move on with life," she said, "to live," she said.

"Move on with life," she said. "There is no life without you," I said.

"Move on with life," she said. "Enjoy our time together," she said.

"Move on with life," she said. "Where do we start?" I asked.

"Move on with life," she said, "and I will tell you," she whispered.

Life Complete

You are what I need to make my life complete

You are what I need to make my life complete, to see the stars at night.

You are what I need to make my life complete, for the sunrise to begin.

You are what I need to make my life complete, with laughter and joy.

You are what I need to make my life complete, to get through the tough
times.

You are what I need to make my life complete, to be at peace in my soul.

You are what I need to make my life complete until I leave this earth.

You are what I need to make my life complete.

When You Speak

When you speak, I try to listen—listen for what you mean, not just what I hear.

When you speak, I try to listen—listen to what you are saying, not just what I hear.

When you speak, I try to listen—listen not to just your words, but for your tones.

When you speak, I try to listen. Why do I try to listen? It is because I find my world rotating around you.

When you speak, I try to listen. Why do I find my world rotating around you? Because I have no other world to travel.

When you speak, I try to listen. Why do I have no other world? Because you are the only world I need.

When you speak, I try to listen. Why will I listen? Because I want to.

Memory of Love

What is the memory of love but a place to go and rest after the storm of life?

Sometimes it is all we have when we are lost with no place to go.

Sometimes it is the pain of life that causes memories to intensify,

Wishing they were real, to almost become alive in our mind's eye.

"Do not flee from me," I shout. "You are all I have left of my love.

You are all I have to keep me warm at night, as she did.

Chase away the shadows of reality; let me rest in your arms once again."

Blessed One Time

I fear that I may never love again, for I have been blessed one time.
Now when I see that chance again, something gets in the way.
Am I haunted by my true love, not wanting to and unable to leave her?
Is she in some distant place, watching out for me, steering me in some
    direction that I know not?
When you experience that one true love, how do you move on?
How can a new love compete with an old one?
Is love simply a fairy tale from now on?
I fear that I may never love again, for I have been blessed one time.

A Curse

I have been refused; I have been turned away, and it hurt.
But I have had the mightiest emotion on earth:
I have been deeply loved by another.
To reject true love is a sin; to accept, a joy;
To remain in that love, a blessing;
To not find it again, a curse.

Heaven and Hell

"What is the difference between heaven and hell?" she asked.
"Love is the difference, true love," he replied.
"What is true love? How will I know?" she asked.
"Do you think that you love me?" he replied.
"Of course I do. Why do you ask?" she said.
"Are you prepared to give up everything you have, even your life?" he
    replied.
After a pause, "I think I would; why?" she asked.
"Because He knew and He did, that's true love," he replied.
"That is the difference between heaven and hell."

Fireworks

As the fireworks go off in the sky, you are with me.
We watched together many times; now I watch alone.
I see your face in the heavens, smiling down at me.
It's almost as if you're saying, "Here I am, watching, guiding you.
You are the reason I watch them, so that I can see you,
So that I can say 'Hello, here I am.' Are you waiting on me
So that I can blow up a kiss? Say 'I miss you'
So that I can say 'I love you.'"

Dreams

A dream is something to be cherished, kept in a place that no one else
    can go to.
Love can be that dream, but is too far way for us to grasp.
It buries itself deep in our hearts, deep in our minds.
We dream in the darkness of night to keep it there.
To see that dream in the light of day would not be the same:
It is only in the dark, in our dreams, that we are free to accept what we
    cannot have in the light of day.

What Would You Be Like?

What would you be like if I were to see you again? I cannot imagine.
Never did I want you to leave me, but you had other roads to travel,
Roads that I could not travel with you.
Would we still have that passion that brought us together to begin with
After we had aged through the years? Would you even recognize me? I
    would you.
Our youth was spent recklessly, never caring for tomorrow, living for
    the day.
Perhaps that is where we went wrong.
I have missed you through the years, wondering from time to time how
    you were, what you were doing; can you say the same?
What would you be like if I were to see you again? I cannot imagine.

Void Between

A love affair that was almost but never was—how does it end?
Should there be shouting? Should there be tears?
How can a heart be broken if it never was whole?
What would have been now never can be.
She was on a level many times above; he, many below.
He wanted her love and nothing else.
She could not make the journey down; he could not make it up.
Plans made could not be carried out; dreams are crushed.
He said, "Please try"; she could not.
Love for both was unfulfilled, the void between too great.

Awaken

As the dawn scratches its way through the night sky,
I awaken to find no one next to me.
You are watching the dawn overcome the night.
Your eyes are closed as if in a dream,
Your body perfectly still as if trying to bring that dream to reality.
As more of the darkness is wiped away by the coming dawn,
You feel that I am near and reach out your hand as if to say *Come here.*
I sit by your side, seeing your beauty awaken.
As the dawn becomes bright in the sky, I lean to kiss your lips.
You smile and say, "Let's go back to bed—I'm getting cold."
As we snuggle in bed, I suddenly awake to realize that it's all been a dream.
I'm alone again.

I Want Nothing

Can you not take a chance and love me?
Can you not get past the feeling of "I don't know"?
Can you live your life alone with no love?
In this winter of my life, I choose not to.
I want to take that chance—I *need* to take that chance.
I want nothing from you but your passion.
I want nothing from you but your warmth on the cold night.
I want nothing from you but your love.

Love Not Shared

What is love if not shared between two people?
It becomes an agony bottled up inside.
It becomes a pounding beat that needs to escape.
If we leave it inside, it turns to something that is not love.
It becomes a bitter feeling, a burning torment.
It becomes a flowing river of pain, not love.
When the surge of pain explodes forth,
Only God knows how to stop it; a man does not.

Insane or Crazy?

Someone asked her, "Are you a little crazy or just plain insane?"
She answered, "Maybe a little of both," and smiled.
I could not help but smile back, for that was the answer I needed to hear.
It matched my own insanity; it said that there was hope for my foolish dream to take hold;
That she understood my pain, my joy, my frustration;
That she understood my need to go on, with my striving not to be something I'm not but only to be what I am.
Someone asked her, "Are you a little crazy or just plain insane?"
She answered, "Maybe a little of both," and smiled.
I said, "Welcome to my world."

PART 3

The Darkness of Life

Darkness

I fear the darkness once again returning, slowly creeping toward me like a fog on the ground.

If I let down my guard, it will overtake me, plunging me to depths that I no longer want to go to,

Not holding my hand in a slow descent but a sudden free fall of unwanted emotion.

Who can stop this? I cannot, though I want to. Who will be there to slow and cushion my sudden plunge downward?

Oh God, please take my hand; let me not see the bottom of the pit as I have before, for it has a floor filled with vipers, striking out, seeking to inflict that fatal bite.

My Dreams

In my dreams, I scream out, *I am, I am, but what am I?*

In my old age, I am not what I thought I would be—

Not an important person; not an athlete, the body too frail.

I no longer believe in fate, for fate has passed me by,

Too afraid of what lies beyond life to let go of my fragile hold on it.

My friend, my love, my wife has gone before me, leaving me empty.

I cannot wake to a different reality, for fate chose this one—I did not.

Nightmare

I cannot awaken from this nightmare called life.
I can only hope that it is a dream gone bad.
The wind in my mind blows heavy, moving those that stand in its way.
I struggle, wanting, *trying* to understand why, but I cannot.
I reach for my pipe and tobacco but cannot grasp it.
Why am I in this down spiral of time? Nothing will wake me.
If you were here, you would wake me
With gentle words, with a soft kiss and a warm embrace.
But you are not here, and I fear for the day,
For I cannot wake from this nightmare called life.

Abandonment

Abandoned by all that we hold dear;
Abandoned by those we loved and thought loved us;
Abandoned by friends, or those we thought were;
Abandoned by all that we hold dear in life, or thought we did;
Abandoned by the earth itself, until that time when we rejoin;
Abandoned—what does it mean? How does it feel?
Abandonment feels like nothing, an emptiness longing to be filled by
    something, by anything, by friends, the warmth of a smile, the
    firmness of a handshake, the closeness of an embrace, the feeling of
    being needed once again.
Abandonment is different for each and yet the same to all: an empty, lost
    feeling of doom.

Is This Death?

Is this what it's like to die? Quiet, no sound, no one lying next to me.
Is this what it's like to die? Awakening from a deep sleep,
Not knowing those first few seconds whether your body is alive.
When I call out, no one answers; no one hears my plea.
No one says good morning; no warmth, no love.
If this is what it is like to die, I want no part of it.

What I Am Not

I cannot be what I am not, though I would be.
Would you, my love, want me to live a lie?
Life is supposed to be warm, full of light, but it cannot be for all.
For some, despair wreaks havoc, with the light being just out of reach.
If we do not accept our role in life, my love, what is to be of us?
Life is like the sea, quiet and beautiful today,
Tomorrow angry and in turmoil. Do we deserve more? I say no.
When we are not what we were meant to be, does that not cause us
    turmoil?
And in turn it causes disappointment and anger when we can't reach that
    light we search for.
I cannot be what I am not, though I would be. Can you?

Unknown

I am unknown to the world, and the world is unknown to me.

What is left for the world to do but to die in that final fiery explosion?

For me, it will be to die in a whimper.

I cannot die in that big explosion; I have no amount of passion left for it to consume—age has consumed it for me.

To be without passion is to be without a reason for life.

If you cannot rekindle passion, what is there but to quietly await the appearance of that shadow known as the Grim Reaper?

I am unknown to the world, and the world is unknown to me.

One Moment

Why do some people laugh when they need to shed tears?

Why do we put on that false face for the world to see while we are broken on the inside?

Are we too ashamed to shed ours tears in public? Are we too ashamed to watch them?

Can we not show our love for them without feeling ashamed or guilty? Must our tears always be in private, behind closed doors?

When a heart is in pain for whatever reason, can we not offer a hug? It's only one moment of compassion, and then you can go back to your life.

I can only guess at what that one moment would cost us, and what that one moment would mean to them.

Why Do You?

Why the hell do you want me to stay around?
You say you want me to be your friend, but when we plan to do something,
    at the last minute you cancel.
I am mystified: how can we be friends doing that? I would prefer that we
    were lovers, but that too is hard to see.
Would it not be less cruel to simply say, *"Go away"*? Would that not be
    more gentle than this?
You were warm, open, and inviting when we first met, but that has gone
    away—I fear never to return again.
Why the hell do you what me to stay around?

Restless Soul

Oh, you unceasingly restless soul, why are you this way?
Why are you not thankful enough for what you have?
Why do you travel far from home and then wonder why you are there?
I understand you not, even though you are in me.
Accept it: you are old and failing, not the youth of years ago—
And yet you still dream of far-off places to go, yearning for the road,
Once again to hear the motor humming out its bass tune while the tires
    join in the concert.
Are you at ease no place but behind the wheel or in that high silver bird?
Could you not as easily escape your stagnate reality of life in a dream?
"One more trip, just that one more trip," your soul yells out.
When and where will it be?

My Mind

My mind will not be silent; the voices shout loudly and will not be quiet.
The myriad of noise continues morning till night.
To think clearly requires a gigantic effort but often is interrupted by the
    sounds and screams of the voices.
Sleep comes only after tossing from side to side for hours.
Silence would be a blessing unknown to me.
To be at peace would be a blessing, but peace does not come.
Is there nothing that a mere mortal can do?
Do the gods on Olympus not hear my cries for help?
Voices, quiet your shouting; let there be peace in my mind.

Who Am I?

I don't know who I am anymore. Could it be I am not?
I want to be *this*, but I am more *that*.
I could be the other but cannot see my way to get there.
Why is life not simple anymore? I cannot say.
Is it the world that is in turmoil, or me?
I was told old age was the golden years; how can it be?
The body begins to fail; the mind begins to slow.
This age of grace suddenly is no more.
I do not like living alone but can find no companion willing.
Is this my fate, to live this winter of my life alone and then die?

Distant

Why has your heart grown so distant, so cold? I don't understand.

When we first met, you wanted closeness and warmth.

No more do I get the feeling that was there when we spent that first night
together.

You brought understanding and desire to our bed; where have they gone?

For myself, I miss the excitement and desire that you had.

Why has it gone away? Why could it not stay?

I have no answer but the quiet loneliness that it has left.

Reality

What is the reality that we all build for ourselves?

Is it better than the dreamworld that we want to live in?

Should we cross over from time to time to see what the other side is like,
or should we stay in our dreams and not let reality interfere with
them?

While the journey out of our dreams seems like a sweet idea, more often
than not it ends in heartache and disaster.

Why do we do this to ourselves? Can we learn from the past not to make
the same mistakes?

Why can you not stay in dreamland and not awake to find her departed,
to find that you are back to that same sad, dry reality that you lived
yesterday?

Never, never will I leave my dreams again; never, never will I seek
something that I don't deserve.

To dream, evermore not to awake, is my goal; reality is not where I want
to live my life anymore.

Sum Total

I am the sum total of many things, some good, some bad.
What is your makeup? Are you more of the good or more of the bad?
I have done things in the past that would shock you.
I have also tried to do some good but failed many times.
But those times when I succeeded are moments that I try to remember—
Those are the warm, fuzzy times that have meant something to me.
What times have you had?
Does the warm and fuzzy stand out more than the cold and disappointing?
Don't forget the bad times; learn from them as much or more than when
    you do good,
For those are the times that we ought not repeat again.
Unfortunately, we often do.

I Waited

I waited for the call that never came. Why did it fail me?
My phone was ready. Maybe she sent an email, but no.
It is late, and still I cannot hear the phone call to me to answer.
Why must the silence be so loud? Why cannot my thoughts be quiet?
I must now know that she has forgotten me; is it just for tonight or for all
    time?
My phone cannot tell me the answer.
It is quiet.

Turned Cold

The weather turned cold when you said goodnight.
You said goodnight when you really meant goodbye.
How did I know? I could look through into the phone to see your face.
You said that I was upset, but you could not have known because of the
    smile I put on my face.
It is but a small thing to you, I know, but it turned my world upside down.
Tomorrow, what it will bring is unknown to most but known to me.
A return to loneliness is my pathway; without love, without hope,
With no one to care.

Abandon This World

I want to abandon this world: it is a harsh, cruel place with little humanity.
I want to abandon this world, for it has no more meaning for me nor
    compassion.
I want to abandon this world, for its beauty has become mired in ugliness
    and hatred.
I want to abandon this world, for human preys upon human with no room
    for pity.
I want to abandon this world: it brings me no comfort or joy.
I want to abandon this world, for loneliness fills my soul with torment
    and pain.
I want to abandon this world, for there is no one to talk with.
I want to abandon this world, for there is no one to embrace.
I want to abandon this world, for there is no one to love.
I want to abandon this world and go to the world my dreams take me.
I want to abandon this world and go to where I will have peace.

Did You Cry?

I am gone, and you are still here. Did you cry? Did you even notice?
I wanted to stay with you, to live our lives together; did you? I think not.
I am far too old to wait for you to think about it.
Sometimes when we see that one thing we want, we need to jump in.
It's nice to wade out slowly into the stream when we're young.
Sometimes it's a one-way conversation, and that's when the talking stops.
When you reach out your hand and it comes back empty, you learn not to
    reach for the impossible anymore.

If You Call

If you call and I don't answer, whom does it hurt more?
Me, I believe; somehow, I don't think you care for me as I do you.
You have to hurt to care. and you do not hurt for me, I think.
I cannot go on caring for you as I do when I don't think you do for me.
I am too old and have had too many heartaches not to notice.
Why do I hang on? What makes me hope beyond hope that there is
    something there that I do not see?
When will I have been tortured enough by my own heart and see that I
    must leave?
Are all loves in old age cursed to start like this?
If you call and I don't answer, whom does it hurt more?

Too Busy

You were too busy to listen to me.

You said you knew me, what I was about, but you didn't.

You said you knew my insecurities, what I had been through, but you didn't.

I tried to tell you what I felt, what I wanted, what I needed, but you didn't listen.

You were too busy talking about yourself, your family, and what a great person you were.

Yes, you had been through hardships, and so had I, but you didn't listen.

Mine were insignificant compared to yours, but not to me.

Then I became insignificant to you; I could not be meaningful to your future.

That was because I was not meaningful to your past.

I Must Lie in It

The bed that I made on my way to here, I must lie in now,

Cold, empty, broken-down, and lonely as it is.

Lovers have fled me as I aged, and night has come on in my life.

I take no joy in how I got here, for there was none to be had.

If only I could have watched from afar, perhaps it would be different.

Perhaps I would have made a bed of flowers to comfort me in my old age.

Perhaps there would be joy, warmth, comfort, and a companion.

But tonight, it has been made and I must lie in it.

Dark Place

Is there no one to hear the plea? Is there no one to answer the cry made in the middle of the night?

Where is that dark place without light that is only reached by turning within?

What do you do when there is no one to turn to for comfort and solace?

Do you turn even more toward the place of no light, toward that dark place you cannot escape from?

To turn toward the blinding light is not possible, for that way you cannot see where your path leads, since there is no one to help lead you.

Keep going, the voices say; *feel your way crawling on the roughshod path that leads down.*

The laughing gets louder the farther downward you plunge.

The voices get louder, louder, saying, *You foolish mortal, did you not think we saw your failures, did you not think we saw the people you left by the wayside?*

And now we leave you by that same wayside, all alone with no one to turn to, all alone with no place to go.

Enjoy this dark place—you will never see the light again.

Silence

Silence is not my friend—it is my nightmare.

Silence is not my friend, for it comes with a price.

Silence is not my friend, for it means I have not heard your voice.

Silence is not my friend, for it means I have seen only your shadows.

Silence is not my friend, for your smile is not with me.

Silence is not my friend, for your laughter is silent.

Silence is not my friend, for I cannot feel your embrace.

Silence is not my friend—no, not my friend at all.

Faded Memories

Why has the distance become so great between us?

It was only yesterday that we enjoyed an embrace, a kiss during that evening when we forgot ourselves, left behind our fears, our troubles, and became as one.

Was it you or I who pushed away, who drew back from the cusp, never to have those feelings again?

Was it uncertainty; was it guilt? Could we not trust ourselves to go forward?

We will never know: we can't take that chance; others have come between.

That night has turned to day, the day to night, and now only faded memories remain as the distance grows greater.

Why Do I Cry?

Why do I cry? It is over you.

Why do I cry? It is over you, for you need me no more.

Why do I cry? It is over you, for you want me no more.

Why do I cry? It is over you, for your embrace is no more.

Why do I cry? It is over you, for your smile is no more.

Why do I cry? It is over you, for your warmth has turned cold.

Why do I cry? It is over you, for you have found another.

Why Do You Come?

Goodbye, goodbye, why do you come? Can you not stay away?

Goodbye, goodbye, why do you come? Can it be easier to say than "Stay awhile longer"?

Goodbye, goodbye, why do you come? You make me afraid of what you hold.

Goodbye, goodbye, why do you come? Are you truly the end of something important for life?

Goodbye, goodbye, why do you come? Are you the end or the beginning of a new life?

Goodbye, goodbye, why do you come? I am not yet ready for the old to leave.

Goodbye, goodbye, why do you come? The shadows of the old have not faded but flicker in the night.

Goodbye, goodbye, why do you come? Will my heart remain to see the shadows fade to nothing, or will my heart fade with them?

Goodbye, goodbye, why do you come? When will you leave me alone?

Bridge to Nowhere

What can I say that has not already been said?

What can I do that has not already been done?

Where can I go that I have not been?

I cannot say what you will not hear.

I cannot do what you won't have done.

I cannot go where you will not follow.

To say what you cannot hear is like talking to an empty room.

To do what you won't have done is like building a bridge to nowhere.

To go where you will not go is my loneliness.

I Cannot See You

Though I want to, I cannot see you tomorrow.

Though you are my life, I must learn to live without you.

Though you joke about it, family and friends would never accept me,

Would ridicule you for making the choice.

Though I think you care, I know it's not as much as I do.

Though I want to hold on and hope, it would bring you pain for me to
do so.

Though to say goodbye would bring me pain, sometimes it is the only
way forward.

May your journeys through the universe bring you the joy and happiness
that I will not have.

Goodbye

When I said goodbye, you said you cried.

I could not cry, for I knew it was over.

I could not cry, since I felt not even friendship anymore.

It was difficult from the start, trying to mold myself to your needs.

It was difficult being something I was not meant to be.

I could not go on knowing I needed to leave.

But was this not the best for both of us, to start again?

When I said goodbye, you said you cried.

I did not.

Needs

My need is not what you need or want; that saddens me greatly,
For I would have given you all that I had, but that was not enough.
I need companionship, a feeling of being wanted, a feeling of love.
You need the comforts that you have become accustomed to that I cannot
　　supply.
What can I say that will make a difference? That I do not know.
Are you too far out of reach for me to obtain?
Must I again travel the road by myself, or can you ever consent to go along
　　with me?
I so much want not to start this journey again alone, for to be alone takes
　　me to places I do not want or need to go,
But I know my need is not what you need or want, and that saddens me
　　greatly.

Death Is My Enemy

Death is the great separator of friends and lovers.
We live, we die, but what of those we leave behind?
Do we love those that we lived with any less? In many ways, we love them
　　more.
We reach out, we call their name, in the night we dream of what was.
We want one last night, one last day: *come back to my life*.
Oh death, you are my enemy; do not take them from us.

Angels

In the distance a siren sounds, moving closer and closer.

It suddenly stops, and the angels that gather the living and the dead, descend.

They are gentle with those who will remain on this earth; there is no need for so much gentleness with those who are already not here.

Now more sirens make their way toward me, and many await their arrival.

They rush from body to body, checking for any signs of those who are the living, not knowing what they will find.

When will they get to me? What will they find, what will they say?

I am cold; I want to go to sleep, but will I awake? And still I wait.

At last, they are next to me; I hear them say, "He didn't make it."

Was that for me or the person next to me? Please tell me I am still here.

They move past, on to the next body. I want to yell out, *I am still with you,* but can not.

Then I realize that the words I heard were for me, and I am not here anymore.

Now I await the coming of different angels.

Do You Believe?

Do you believe in love? I used to; I wonder now.

My love has left me to travel where I cannot go.

I no longer can sleep at ease through the night

For she is not there beside me.

The mornings are cold and empty now; the nights more so.

Till we are rejoined in the great beyond,

Watch over me; guide me as you did when you were here.

A Reason

There must be a reason, but I don't know what it is:
A reason I need to let you go, why you can't stay.
Maybe there's someone else for you to be with.
Maybe I'm more of a fool than I thought, thinking you would stay.
I know that I want you to; I know that you will not.
My world will not be the same; it will be lonely when you leave.
You were an explosion of desire for a brief moment.
You were the center of my world for such a short time.
There must be a reason you will go, but I don't know what it is.

Why?

Why doesn't the phone ring when we truly need it?
Why can't the voice on the other end bring comfort?
Why is it robocall after robocall, and not the one you want to hear from?
Why does it want to sell me insurance, jewelry, all the things I don't need?
Not what I do need.
Why can it not be silent, no text asking me to say something that I don't
        want to?
Why can I not get that call from the voice that I want to hear?
Why, why must there be only silence and no comfort?
Why, oh why is it so hard to accept the silence from the one you want,
The one you need to hear from?

Which Part?

Which part of me do you want the most, the part that wants to stay or the
part that you want to go away?
The part that stays wants to be your friend, your lover, your life's blood.
The part of me that you want to go away would be battered and broken
to do so.
I know I am not your dream man, the love of your life, but it is not good
to live into the winters of our lives alone, with no one to hold hands
with, embrace, and share passion with.
When you don't want to talk, I'll be there holding you. When you hurt,
so will I, but I'll rub your feet to get the soreness out.
When you are sick, I'll fix you chicken soup or toast to calm your stomach.
When you want to dance, I'll try not to step on your toes with my clumsy
feet.
We will drink wine and sit on the deck, remembering old times and
dreaming of the new ones.
Call it lust, passion, or love, I know not which it is—I call it life.

Not the Same

The night is not the same with you not beside me.
When I look to your empty spot next to me, it is cold and cruel in its
silence.
Why did you leave so suddenly, without goodbyes?
There were words that needed to be said, embraces that needed to be felt.
To sleep is not the same with this emptiness beside me.
When I reach out to feel your body, to watch you breathe, there is nothing.
If only you could magically return to me, softly in the night, my life would
be complete.
Why can I not even dream of you? Why do you stay away even from that?
Is this my pain, is this my penance, living this lonely life without you?
Come to me: bring the comfort that I so desperately seek;
Release me free from this empty plain of life so that my sleep may once
again be peaceful.

Deafening Silence

For there to be a day without your voice is a deafening silence.

To not hear from you is an unbearable injustice.

Your voice is like a sweet symphony to my ears:

Soft violins, muted brass, gently saying that you are still with me even
though far away.

Why do you delay in calling my name? Busy as you may be, the delay only
deepens the need to hear you.

I know that you do not have the time or need to hear mine, and that only
adds to my sad waiting to hear you say, "Hello, it's me."

Will there ever be a day that we need not wait to hear our voices unite to
form a majestic orchestra of passion to be played together?

I know that the wait for this question to be answered will be long, but wait
I will, as you are the one worth the time.

Eternal Question

The cold air from the north slowly settles in.

The first flakes of snow fill the winter air.

I can only guess what tomorrow will bring.

This is not a life that I chose,

But one fate has unfolded before me:

To be alone is not how one should live.

When you have no one to share breakfast with,

No person next to you to say goodnight,

The air is almost as cold as the loneliness within.

The need is there, but the companionship is not.

Is this my last winter in this place of sorrow?

Only God can answer this eternal question.

The Tear I Cry

I cry a tear, for I am alone in this world.
Not that I want to be, but my love has left me.
I am unable to find love again, but not for trying.
Those who say, "I need you," really don't; why?
To be held close again is but a dream.
To feel that passion in a long kiss I have not felt.
My days are now shorter than when I was young.
They seemed endless then, with time for anything.
But now I have no time to spare, no endless time.
Perhaps the tear I cry is for that; I may never know.

Oh, What a Dream!

Awakened by a dream—oh, what a dream it was!
Full of death that was not of death to come,
Not of death unknown but of death known,
Not that of a stranger but that of family,
What was that dream trying to say to me?
What message was it trying to deliver from the grave?
What can I do to help bring him peace?
What can I do to help him sleep that eternal sleep?
What can I do to sleep here on this earth,
To awaken from this dream no more?

PART 4

Reflections

Glass of Water

My life is like the glass partially filled with water. But instead of being half full, it's more like a quarter filled, for it is the winter of my life. Spring, summer, and fall have passed. I find myself alone, as I was in the spring of my life. But this time it is without promise, without stamina, and most important without time. Those who read this will say, "You've led a good life," and yes, I have been blessed. But what is life in the winter of your years without a companion? Someone you can talk to, that you can be warm with, in front of a fire on those cold nights and make love with.

I enter this season of my life with some uncertainty about what this season holds for me. I tell myself that I am not going to pass from this world till I am 104 years old. Don't laugh too hard—that's my goal. We each do our best to adjust in our winters—some with great success, others struggling with the changes that come with aging.

May your struggles be quickly over and peace find you wherever you go. May the winds favor your sails on a smooth sea. May God know of you.

Expectations

As we age, our dreams, expectations, and goals change. People come and go, jobs change, loved ones pass from this world. There is only one constant in our lives while we are here: God. How we choose to accept him makes all the difference.

Some say there is no God, and does that mean we are free to do as we please? Some say there is a God, and does that mean we are above others and perfect? What if either side is wrong? What does it really cost to lead a good life and do the right thing? Nothing.

If you say there is no God and you're right, to do good and lead a life of service costs nothing. If there is a God—and I say there is—if we choose to ignore him and what he expects, in the short term it may cost us nothing, but what does it cost in the long term?

This Life

In this life, there are few things that are truly important, that stay with us. The first in life is our parents, for they gave us life and then a meaning to that life. Then our teachers taught us words and concepts and how to use them. Our friends during those school years were important, but where are they now?

Our first love taught us what passion was—what it meant, we thought, to be in love. Our spouse then taught us what real love was about, but unfortunately many did not learn that lesson well. Our jobs tried to teach us responsibility; again, some did not learn that well, either.

Through it all, we had one constant thing in our lives: our God, by whatever name you called him. He was always there through victories and failings, but again some either forgot or didn't learn this lesson well.

Each lesson in our lives we should learn from, take to heart, and not forget. But few do. Will you be one?

Intersection

What to do when life comes to an intersection, and you take an unexpected turn to a direction that was not foreseen? Can you ever retrace those steps that brought you to this point in life, or are they lost forever? I found out this morning that they are lost, never to be reclaimed, never to bring back happiness. That is a cruel lesson to learn when you least expect it.

Can something be wanted so badly that it brings disaster? Can a relationship be wanted so badly that it is doomed to fail? I am here to tell you that yes, it can.

Plain Laziness

Friends, friends, and friends: can you remember all the friends you made in a lifetime? I cannot. We went our separate ways, each with a different road to travel, each with a different destiny to live out, with a different fate in the end.

Why did we lose touch with one another? We did not have the technology when I got out of school. It was easy to say, "I'll see you later," and then forget. Today to stay in touch is easy. Open up your computer, email someone half a world away. Open up your phone and call that same person. But yet we still say goodbye too easily. Why? Do we not value those who call us friends? Is it that we don't have the physical contact? Is that what we need to remember?

Speaking as someone who is at least as guilty as anyone else, who has traveled the world on business and pleasure and met thousands of people, I think it is just plain laziness.

Life and Passion

What does passion bring to life? A desire for success, a desire for sex? Perhaps, but I think as we get older it comes down to being with others, and that's what brings us happiness in life. Success, by my age, has come and gone, and sex isn't far behind. But to lie next to someone who is warm and not expecting more than to be held close, to rub their back and say soft things in the middle of the night—I think that is the true passion of life. At seventy-two, I can think of nothing more to ask for than this.

Renewed Hope

Renewed hope means what? New dreams? The breath that has been held in for so long can finally be exhaled?

But can hope leave as quickly as it arrived? What do we do, what can we do, to overcome that terrible feeling when that happens? When that sweet breath of fresh air that our lungs longed for is brief, and we exhale that sweet breath, realizing that our hope was but a brief respite from pain and hurt ...

It has a sharp sting, like a thousand hornets. Is this how we are to end up? Swollen from the stings, unable to breathe that sweet fresh air of hope, unable to understand, not wanting to understand how that one brief moment of hope came and went so quickly.

What Is Love?

What is love if we do not feel it in our very being, not only in our heart? Is love possible at first sight? Is love possible after one's love has passed? What will a new love be like? Do we slip back to the old one, trying to not let go, or jump with both feet into a new one, not forgetting the old?

Can we understand the difference between the two, or are we locked in confusion between them? Will the feelings be the same, or will the disappointments be the same and hurt as much?

The Struggle

During a heavy storm, amid the rain blowing wildly, you will hear a great struggle going on—a struggle between the fierce wind and the old guard trees that have stood for decades. The wind wants the trees to break apart and kiss the ground. The trees say, "No, I will shed some branches, but I will fight you as long as you are here." The wind says, "I am mightier than you and will blow you over." The trees usually win, but sometimes you hear a loud groan that happens when the wind has won. It is almost imperceptible at first. Then it becomes louder as the tree knows it has lost. The loud roar and sudden crash to the ground signal the end of the battle.

Perhaps this is how we feel when we lose a loved one. We battle to say, "No, no, I will not let this happen," and when it does, we feel that sudden crash of absence. We know the battle is lost, but unlike the trees, we cannot just quit. The pain will not let us. But in time we go on, as the wind does to the next battle, saying we will not lose this time—though in our hearts, we know we will.

We all fight this fight, knowing in the end that all will be right in God's world.

Alone

What is true aloneness? Is it on an island where you are the only person, or could it be in the big city, surrounded by countless people who are afraid to say hello, afraid to accept a kind word?

I think it is the sadness that is the ultimate feeling of aloneness: far from family, but close to people who are strangers and who are afraid to commit to being your friends.

All our adult lives we try to be with someone—a companion, a spouse, someone to bridge that gap between ourselves and the shadow of loneliness. What do we do when that bridge is suddenly unexpectedly lost, often permanently?

Pipe Smoke

As the gray rings of pipe smoke rise slowly into the air, I think of life's passion, how it is thick at the beginning but slowly leaves us as we age. Is that how love is meant to be, red hot with passion to start, cooling as we age? Some say if it's meant to be, it will, but I say no—as with a small flame at the bottom of a fire, add small pieces till you finally get to large ones, and watch the flames growing ever hotter, ever higher. This is how passion should build, build into love. At the end of life, all should have had that feeling at least once; if you're lucky, twice.

We the People

We the people … well, I'll interpret it to mean we and *some* of the people. Those who have purple polka dots are not in the "we," and I'm not for sure about Sue over there—she doesn't agree with some of my stands. Then there's … oh, I won't get into that.

I guess that narrows down my "we" quite a bit. I guess it really excludes about everyone.

Since you don't agree with me, I guess I'll just rewrite the Constitution and take out the word "we." I'll put in the word "I," since I'm the only one that counts. I like that: "I the people." It's all-inclusive because it includes me and eliminates those I don't like: everybody else.

Now if you believe the above garbage, you have got a problem. The WE stands for everyone. We are Americans first. Understand this, as one person told me: suck it up and get on with life. Vote for the Easter Bunny if you want to write in a name, but vote. Otherwise, you can't complain, because you didn't try and participate in the beginning.

Fate

Sometimes fate plays with us. Sometimes it's bad, sometimes it's good. It appears that I am destined to live my remaining days alone—without the passion of that warm embrace, without the kiss in the morning that says *I'm glad you're here with me.* It has been interesting, what fate has dealt me, playing with my emotions. Through the jokes that it has played on me, I have learned what being alone really feels like. It isn't fun, I can tell you that. But it has taught me another lesson as well: hold tight to those that really love you, for you never, ever know when they might leave you. Kiss them goodnight, give them an extra-long hug, for it might be the last time you can do that.

To Be or Not to Be

To be or not to be is not the question, because you already are. The real question is, How do you want to live life? How do you want to be remembered? What was your purpose, what did you accomplish, and how did you accomplish it?

Do you only have riches and fame? If that was your goal, you have missed life entirely. Sure, a certain degree of money is important, but if you don't have a passion for something and love of a family, surely you are the poorer for it.

As I have grown older, that is what has come to stand out to me after seeing so many people broken down by living a false life, after seeing so many people living a false love, not willing to fix what is broken. They throw it away, start all over with someone else, make the same mistakes again, throw the new one away, start again. It is sad that we have this mentality. What happened to "till death do us part"? Now it's "till I don't like you anymore." What happened to "in sickness and in health"? Now it's till the insurance runs out.

Loyalty is a forgotten word. We often do not show it for family, and not in our work life, either. Greed will be the downfall of society as we know it. Look at the business failures that are increasingly happening, many of them because large corporations gobble up smaller ones and then find that the debt can't be paid by greed. Who suffers? Ordinary people, not the bigwigs.

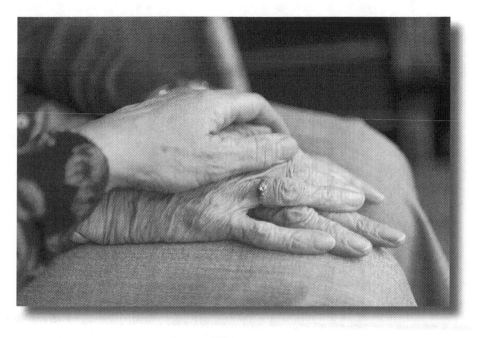

Time

I was asked recently, "Can a broken heart find its way home? Does someone always love you?" That is a question for all eternity. Most broken hearts heal in time. Some take longer than others. They say that time is the great healer, but the question is how much time it takes. I do believe it is always possible for someone to love you. Why, you may ask? Because I had a lady who did. Now, there were times she didn't *like* me too well, but as for loving me, there was no question. May you be so blessed.

Candlesticks

In life, sometimes it takes two pieces of something to make a whole, as with a candlestick and a candle. While each can be used in a different way by itself, they achieve their true purpose only when they unite as one, supporting each other while giving off a light that others can see. That is the way life should be: partners supporting each other through the blood, sweat, tears, and joys that life brings to all of us.

The candle is supported by the candlestick until it has burned down and the light of the flame slowly flickers and quietly dies. Is that not what should happen between two partners?

I think that when one has to start from the beginning, especially at an older age, it is hard. Expectations have changed from our lustful youth to wanting someone simply to talk or share meals with, someone you turn over to in the night to make sure they're OK and occasionally cuddle with. Why is it so hard to start again? Are we so set in our ways that we cannot open up to new relationships and experiences?

Off Button

Life does not respond as we want it to. We can't push a button on life and expect it to react as a computer does. If we could, we would not have the ups and downs that make us human. I'll just punch your off button if I don't like you. But how could we gather our information together if we did that? We need both sides of the information spectrum in order to make an intelligent decision. OK, I know it's hard to tell the right from the wrong these days, but without both sides of what is going on, you make improper decisions. Listen to both the good and the bad. I used to tell the sales people I trained, "Shut up and listen. That is the only way to understand your customer's problem. Think while you listen, you might accidently come up with the right solution." (Pardon the sarcasm.)

Epilogue:
More Than We Are

Why do we want to be more than we are, bigger than what life has planned for us?

Why do we want to be more than we are, to impress those known?

Why do we want to be more than we are, to impress those unknown?

Why do we want to be more than we are? The trouble it brings is not seen but surely comes.

Why do we want to be more than we are? Is life not large enough as it is?

Why do we want to be more than we are? Do not our family and friends like us as we are?

Why do we want to be more than we are? Does the world yell at us ever to be larger than life?

Why do we want to be more than we are? In our youth, it starts slowly and then explodes.

Why do we want to be more than we are? In our old age we sit and wonder why could not we have been satisfied with what we were.

Why do we want to be more than we are? Could it be because God made man with a searching soul?

Why do we want to be more than we are? I will never know. Will you?

Dreams and Lovers

Dreams and lovers should always end in the dead of night
With the lights turned down, so that they cannot see the pain
On the face or hear the soft words that should be said but go unspoken.
How do you say you're sorry for failing to be the answer
For what the other is looking for, failing at love for not fulfilling their
    dreams?
As the sun rises, chasing the stars from the heavens, the moon sets,
Taking with it what once was the dream, the love, and the hope in the
    new day.
There is no peace in body, mind, or soul, only turmoil and sadness that
    begins all over again,
And we ask why, but get no answer.

Printed in the United States
by Baker & Taylor Publisher Services